SMART
ABOUT
SPORTS

Meet the Cubs

By
Mike Kennedy
with Mark Stewart

NORWOOD HOUSE PRESS

Norwood House Press, P.O. Box 316598, Chicago, Illinois 60631

For information regarding Norwood House Press,
please visit our website at: www.norwoodhousepress.com or call 866-565-2900.

Photo Credits:
   Getty (4, 8, 12, 13, 15, 16, 21, 23 bottom), Associated Press (7, 22), Black Book Partners (18, 23 top), Icon SMI (20).
Cover Photos:
   Top Left: Baseball Cards Magazine; Top Right: Jonathan Daniel/Getty Images; Bottom Left: Scott Wachter/Icon SMI;
   Bottom Right: Topps, Inc.
The baseball memorabilia photographed for this book is part of the authors' collection:
   Page 6) Billy Williams: Topps, Inc., Page 10) Cap Anson: Old Judge & Gypsy Queen Cigarettes; Gabby Hartnett: The Exhibit
   Supply Company; Mordecai Brown: The Ramly Company; Ernie Banks: Topps, Inc., Page 11) Fergie Jenkins: Topps, Inc.;
   Ryne Sandberg: Fleer Corp.; Mark Grace: Baseball Cards Magazine; Greg Maddux: Topps, Inc.
Special thanks to Topps, Inc.

Editor: Brian Fitzgerald
Designer: Ron Jaffe
Project Management: Black Book Partners, LLC.
Editorial Production: Jessica McCulloch

LIBRARY OF CONGRESS CATALOGING-IN-PUBLICATION DATA
   Kennedy, Mike (Mike William), 1965-
   Meet the Cubs / by Mike Kennedy with Mark Stewart.
      p. cm. -- (Smart about sports)
   Includes bibliographical references and index.
   Summary: "An introductory look at the Chicago Cubs baseball team. Includes
a brief history, facts, photos, records, glossary, and fun
activities"--Provided by publisher.
   ISBN-13: 978-1-59953-369-8 (library edition : alk. paper)
   ISBN-10: 1-59953-369-3 (library edition : alk. paper)
   1. Chicago Cubs (Baseball team)--Juvenile literature. I. Stewart, Mark,
1960- II. Title.
   GV875.N4K46 2010
   796.357'640977311--dc22
                              2009043044

Manufactured in the United States of America in North Mankato, Minnesota.
N147—012010

Contents

Words in **bold type** are defined on page 24.

The Cubs are happy after a win in 2009.

The Chicago Cubs

Chicago is known as the "Windy City." When the winds blow in the winter, it gets very cold. People in Chicago love when spring arrives each year. That means warmer weather—and the start of a new season for the Cubs! The Cubs are one of baseball's oldest teams. Their fans are very loyal. The Cubs reward them by playing hard and never giving up.

Once Upon a Time

The National League (NL) was born in 1876. The Cubs were members of the NL from the very first day. They were called the White Stockings back then. Later they changed their name to the Cubs.

The Cubs have always put great players on the field. Their famous hitters include Cap Anson, Hack Wilson, Ernie Banks, Billy Williams, Ryne Sandberg, and Sammy Sosa. Their famous pitchers include Mordecai Brown, Fergie Jenkins, and Greg Maddux.

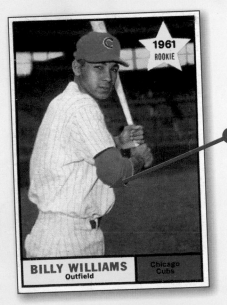

1961 ROOKIE

BILLY WILLIAMS
Outfield

Chicago Cubs

Ernie Banks warms up before practice.

The Cubs play an afternoon game in Wrigley Field.

At the Ballpark

The Cubs play their home games in Wrigley Field. Wrigley Field is famous for having ivy on its walls. Sometimes a ball bounces into the ivy. The outfielder has to find the ball quickly. The Cubs once had a player who was afraid to reach into the ivy. They had to trade him to another team!

Shoe Box

The cards on these pages belong to the authors. They show some of the best Cubs ever.

Cap Anson

First Baseman

• 1876–1897
Cap Anson was a big star in the early days of baseball. He was the first player to reach 3,000 hits.

Gabby Hartnett

Catcher • 1922–1940
Leo "Gabby" Hartnett was a smart and talented player. Some say he was the best catcher ever.

Mordecai Brown

Pitcher

• 1904–1912 & 1916
Mordecai Brown lost parts of two fingers in a farm accident. He was able to make the ball move in strange ways when he threw it.

Ernie Banks

Shortstop

• 1953–1971
Ernie Banks was the most popular player in team history. He was known as "Mr. Cub."

10

Fergie Jenkins

Pitcher

•**1966–1973 & 1982–1983**
Fergie Jenkins was a tall and powerful pitcher. He won at least 20 games six years in a row for the Cubs.

Ryne Sandberg
SECOND BASE

Ryne Sandberg

Second Baseman

• **1982–1994 & 1996–97**
Ryne Sandberg was a great fielder, hitter, and runner. In 1984, "Ryno" won the NL Most Valuable Player (MVP) award.

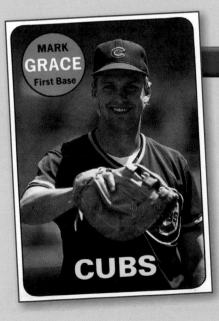

Mark Grace

First Baseman • 1988–2000
Mark Grace batted higher than .300 nine times for the Cubs. He also won four **Gold Glove** awards for his great fielding.

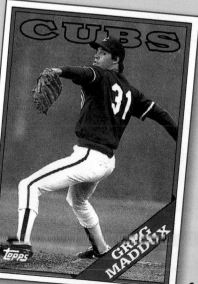

Greg Maddux

Pitcher

• **1986–1992 & 2004–2006**
Scoring a run off of Greg Maddux was very difficult. He could throw his pitches exactly where he wanted.

ABC's of Baseball

In this picture of Derrek Lee, how many things can you find that begin with the letter **C**?

See page 23 for answer.

13

Brain Games

Here is a poem about a great Chicago star:

There once was a Cubbie named Santo,
Who thought, "There is nothing I can't do."
In the field and at bat,
He was quick as a cat,
And from Cubs fans he never heard boo.

Guess which one of these facts is **TRUE**:

- *Ron Santo went on to become an announcer for the Cubs.*

- *Ron once wrestled with a real bear cub.*

See page 23 for answer.

14

Ron Santo practices his hitting before a game.

Sammy Sosa gets a
big cheer from the
"Bleacher Bums."

Fun on the Field

In most ballparks, the best seats are close to home plate. At Wrigley Field, fans like to sit behind the outfield wall, in the bleachers. They call themselves "Bleacher Bums."

A fan who catches a home run hit by a Cub has a treasure for life. When the other team hits a home run, the fan who catches the ball throws it back on the field. Then the crowd always cheers!

On the Map

The Cubs call Chicago, Illinois home. The players come from all over the country— and all over the world. Match these MVPs with the places where they were born:

 1 **Gabby Hartnett** • 1935 NL MVP
Woonsocket, Rhode Island

 2 **Ernie Banks**
• **1958 & 1959 NL MVP**
Dallas, Texas

 3 **Ryne Sandberg** • 1984 NL MVP
Spokane, Washington

 4 **Andre Dawson** • 1987 NL MVP
Miami, Florida

 5 **Sammy Sosa** • 1998 NL MVP
San Pedro de Macoris,
Dominican Republic

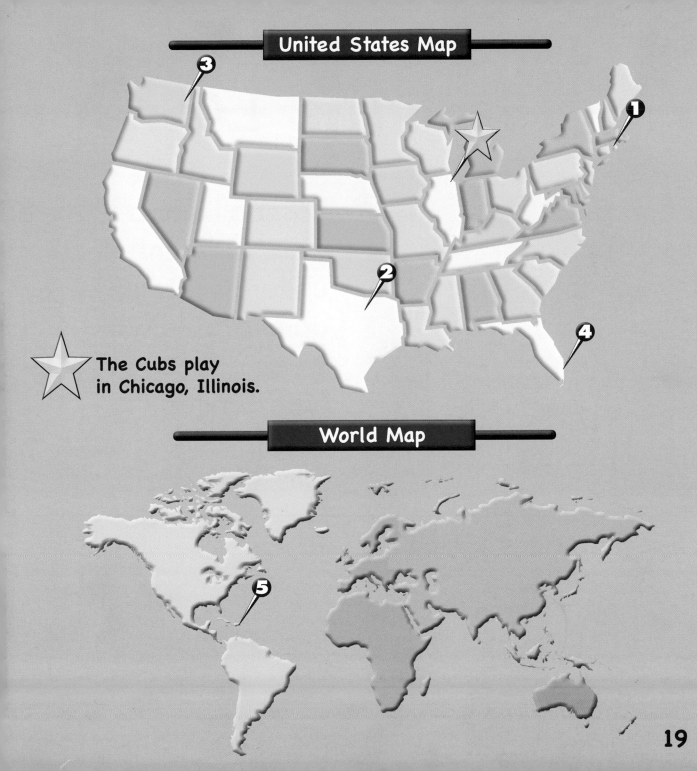

United States Map

The Cubs play in Chicago, Illinois.

World Map

19

What's in the Locker?

Baseball teams wear different uniforms for home games and away games. Chicago's home uniform is bright white. It has thin, blue stripes called pinstripes. The uniform top has the team name inside a circle.

Ryan Theriot wears the team's home uniform.

Chicago's away uniform is gray. The uniform top spells out **C-H-I-C-A-G-O**. The players wear a cap with the letter **C** on the front.

Aramis Ramirez wears the team's road uniform.

We Won!

In 1907 and 1908, the Cubs won the World Series. Fans in Chicago expected many more championships. But as the years passed, the Cubs fell short time and again. They had many great players and teams. But something always kept the Cubs from winning it all. Still, their fans have never stopped rooting for them. They love the Cubs, win or lose.

Three Cubs jump for joy.

22

Record Book

These Cubs stars set amazing team records.*

Hitter	Record	Year
Rogers Hornsby	.380 **Batting Average**	1929
Hack Wilson	191 **Runs Batted In**	1930
Sammy Sosa	66 Home Runs	1998

Pitcher	Record	Year
Mordecai Brown	29 Wins	1908
Fergie Jenkins	274 Strikeouts	1970
Randy Myers	53 **Saves**	1993

* All records set since 1900.

Answer for ABC's of Baseball
Here are words in the picture that start with **C**:
Cap, Catcher, Cheek, Chicago Cub, Crowd.
Did you find any others?

Answer for Brain Games
The first fact is true. Ron Santo started announcing Cubs games in 1990. He also hit 342 home runs and won five Gold Glove awards for the team.

Baseball Words

BATTING AVERAGE
A measure of how often a batter gets a hit. A .300 average is very good.

GOLD GLOVE
An award given to players who are very good fielders.

RUNS BATTED IN
The number of runners that score on a batter's hits and walks.

SAVES
A number that shows how many times a pitcher comes into a game and completes a win for his team.

Index

Photos are on **bold** numbered pages.

About the Cubs

Learn more about the Cubs at chicago.cubs.mlb.com

Learn more about baseball at www.baseballhalloffame.org